TUDOR
1485–1603
STUART
1603–1714
GEORGIAN
1714–1837
VICTORIAN
1837–1901
MODERN TIMES
1901–NOW
AF476911

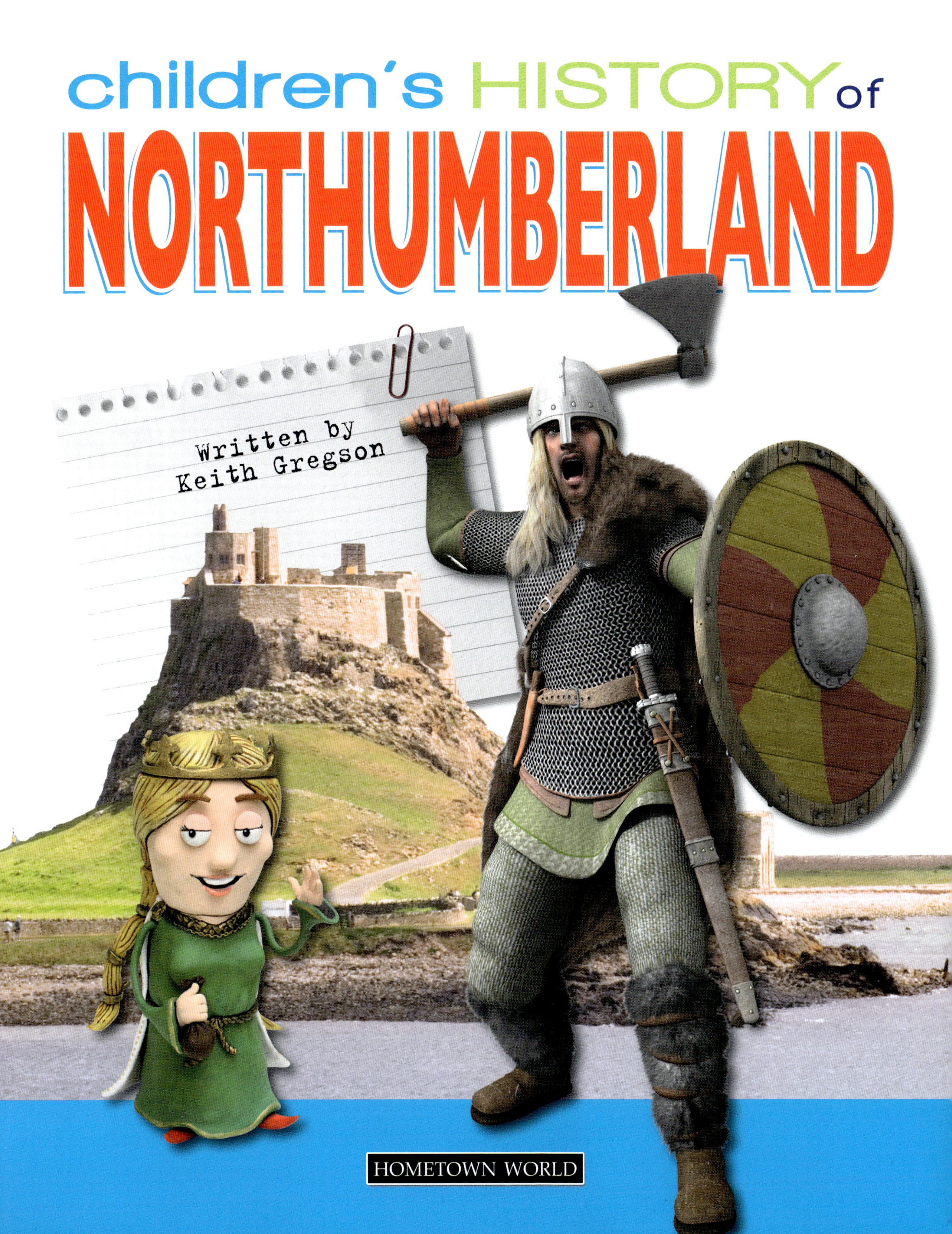

children's HISTORY of
NORTHUMBERLAND
Written by
Keith Gregson
HOMETOWN WORLD

How well do you know Northumberland?

Have you ever wondered what it would have been like living in Northumberland when the Romans built Hadrian's Wall? What about living in a pele tower? This book will uncover the important and exciting things that happened in Northumberland.

Want to hear the other good bits? Some rather brainy folk have worked on this book to make sure it's fun and informative. So what are you waiting for? Peel back the pages and be amazed at what happened near your town or village.

Timeline shows which period (dates and people) each spread is talking about

Intriguing photos

THE FACTS

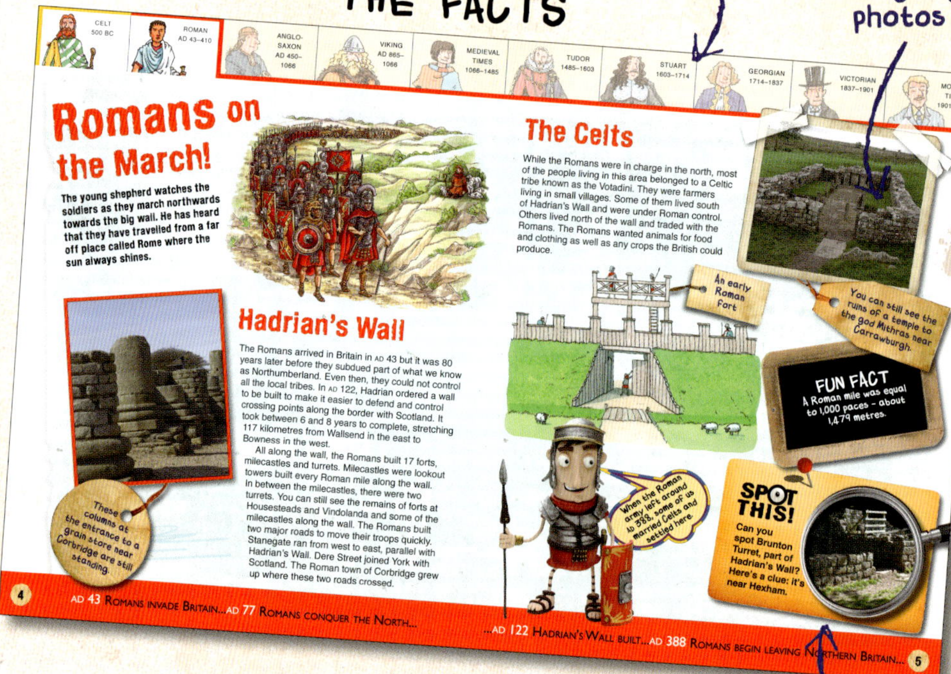

THE EVIDENCE

Fun facts to amaze you!

'Spot this!' game with hints on something to find near you

An imaginary account of what it was like for children growing up in Northumberland

A summary explaining how we know about the past

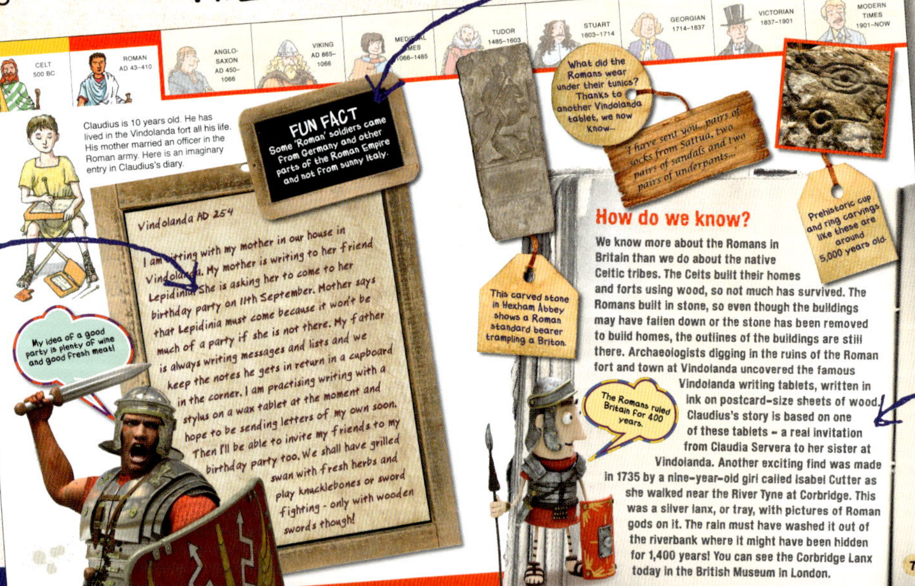

VIKING
MEDIEVAL TIMES
TUDOR
STUART
GEORGIAN
VICTORIAN
MODERN TIMES
AD 800   AD 900   1000   1100   1200   1300   1400   1500   1600   1700   1800   1900   2000

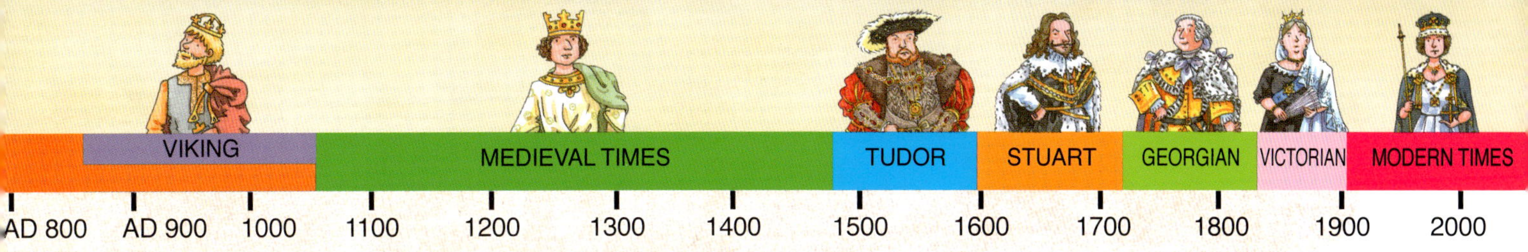

Contents

Romans on the March!

The young shepherd watches the soldiers as they march northwards towards the big wall. He has heard that they have travelled from a far off place called Rome where the sun always shines.

Hadrian's Wall

The Romans arrived in Britain in AD 43 but it was 80 years later before they subdued part of what we know as Northumberland. Even then, they could not control all the local tribes. In AD 122, Hadrian ordered a wall to be built to make it easier to defend and control crossing points along the northern frontier. It took between 6 and 8 years to complete, stretching 117 kilometres from Wallsend in the east to Bowness in the west.

All along the wall, the Romans built 17 forts, milecastles and turrets. Milecastles were lookout towers built every Roman mile along the wall. In between the milecastles, there were two turrets. You can still see the remains of forts at Housesteads and Vindolanda and some of the milecastles along the wall. The Romans built two major roads to move their troops quickly. Stanegate ran from west to east, parallel with Hadrian's Wall. Dere Street joined York with the far north. The Roman town of Corbridge grew up where these two roads crossed.

Columns at the entrance to a Roman grain store near Corbridge are still standing.

AD **43** Romans invade Britain...AD **77** Romans conquer the North...

The Celts

While the Romans were in charge in the north, most of the people living in this area belonged to a Celtic tribe known as the Votadini. They were farmers living in small villages. Some of them lived south of Hadrian's Wall and were under Roman control. Others lived north of the wall and traded with the Romans. The Romans wanted animals for food and clothing as well as any crops the British could produce.

An early Roman fort

You can still see the ruins of a temple to the god Mithras near Carrawburgh.

FUN FACT

A Roman mile was equal to 1,000 paces – about 1,479 metres.

SPOT THIS!

Can you spot Brunton Turret, part of Hadrian's Wall? Here's a clue: it's near Hexham.

Claudius is 10 years old. He has lived in the Vindolanda fort all his life. His mother married an officer in the Roman army. Here is an imaginary entry in Claudius's diary.

FUN FACT

Some 'Roman' soldiers came from Germany and other parts of the Roman Empire and not from sunny Italy.

Vindolanda AD 254

I am sitting with my mother in our house in Vindolanda. My mother is writing to her friend Lepidinia. She is asking her to come to her birthday party on 11th September. Mother says that Lepidinia must come because it won't be much of a party if she is not there. My father is always writing messages and lists and we keep the notes he gets in return in a cupboard in the corner. I am practising writing with a stylus on a wax tablet at the moment and hope to be sending letters of my own soon. Then I'll be able to invite my friends to my birthday party too. We shall have grilled swan with fresh herbs and play knucklebones or sword fighting - only with wooden swords though!

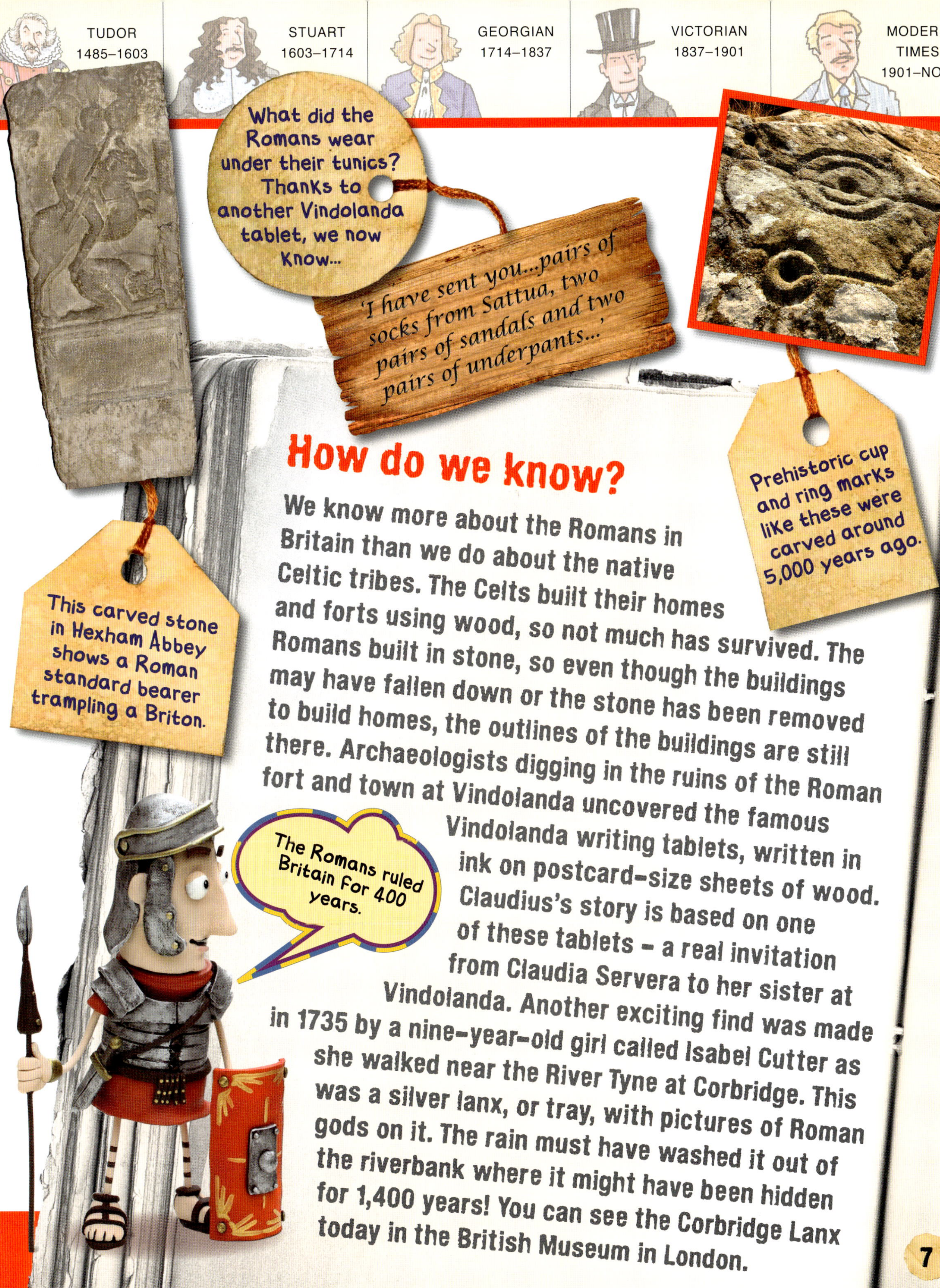

How do we know?

We know more about the Romans in Britain than we do about the native Celtic tribes. The Celts built their homes and forts using wood, so not much has survived. The Romans built in stone, so even though the buildings may have fallen down or the stone has been removed to build homes, the outlines of the buildings are still there. Archaeologists digging in the ruins of the Roman fort and town at Vindolanda uncovered the famous Vindolanda writing tablets, written in ink on postcard-size sheets of wood. Claudius's story is based on one of these tablets – a real invitation from Claudia Servera to her sister at Vindolanda. Another exciting find was made in 1735 by a nine-year-old girl called Isabel Cutter as she walked near the River Tyne at Corbridge. This was a silver lanx, or tray, with pictures of Roman gods on it. The rain must have washed it out of the riverbank where it might have been hidden for 1,400 years! You can see the Corbridge Lanx today in the British Museum in London.

New Kingdom

The rain beats down on the weary travellers as night begins to fall. But young Ahlfrith and his family are happy. They have just visited Holy Cuthbert on Holy Island and have been blessed by him. Now they are on their long journey home through the Northumbrian hills. They will ask this stranger if they can shelter here for the night.

Map of Angle-Land AD 600-900

This map shows the Anglo-Saxon Kingdoms in AD 600-900.

Northumbria

When the Romans left Britain, new invaders arrived. In AD 547 the Angle chief, Ida the Flamebearer, raided the coast and conquered the stronghold at Bamburgh. His kingdom became known as Bernicia.

The Angles settled in small villages of wooden huts surrounded by wooden fences and a ditch to keep out wild animals and invaders. The chief, or 'thegn', lived in a big hall. Bernicia had another stronghold at Ad Gefrin near Yeavering, with a royal palace and big meeting house. But these were not peaceful times. The kingdom had to be defended from the Celts in the north and west, and the Saxons in the south. Twice, Ad Gefrin was burnt down.

Ida's grandson, Aethelfrith, who ruled around AD 600, married Acha from the next-door kingdom of Deira. This was the beginning of Northumbria – one of the most powerful kingdoms in Britain. Northumbria got its name because it was north of the River Humber.

...AD 547 ANGLES INVADE...AD 604 BERNICIA AND DEIRA UNITED AS NORTHUMBRIA...

A Holy Island

In AD 627, a monk called Paulinus arrived in Ad Gefrin and began teaching the people of Bernicia about Christianity. Aethelfrith's son, Oswald, became a Christian. When he became king of Northumbria he invited a monk called Aidan to start a monastery at Lindisfarne on Holy Island. Aidan built a wooden monastery. Although he died in AD 651 the monastery carried on.

Northumbria's most famous saint, Cuthbert, was a shepherd boy in Scotland and a soldier before coming to Holy Island. People believed that Cuthbert could work miracles. He died in AD 687 and the monks carried his body with them wherever they went to keep it safe. Today it lies in Durham Cathedral.

Battle of Heavenfield

Around this time, Northumbria was attacked again, this time by Mercia. Northumbria was split into Bernicia and Deira again. When Oswald took over and won a great victory at the Battle of Heavenfield in about AD 634 Northumbria was reunited.

Edwina is a 10-year-old girl. She lives in a small village in the hills of Northumbria. Edwina and her family have been on a pilgrimage to Lindisfarne to see Saint Cuthbert. Here is an imaginary account from Edwina.

20th March, AD 667

I'm really tired now! It has been a long journey from our little village to Lindisfarne but Dad says that I will never forget it. On the way there, we had a short rest while we waited for the tide to go out before walking across to Holy Island. I liked Cuthbert – he's really good with animals. He used to be a shepherd just like me! He told me how to be careful with the eider ducks when they are on their nests. We're going to call our eider ducks 'cuddy ducks' from now on, after Cuthbert. The island was packed with people like us and I'm not surprised. Everyone's heard stories about Cuthbert being able to heal sick people and do miracles. He gave us a blessing before we set off home. I'm glad to be back in one piece – now that's a miracle!

English	God
Monday	Moon's day
Tuesday	Tiw's day
Wednesday	Woden's day
Thursday	Thor's day
Friday	Freya's day
Saturday	Saturn's day
Sunday	Sun's day

Many of the days of the week come from the names of old Anglo-Saxon gods.

FUN FACT
Northumbria has its own language that comes from Old English.

A page from the Lindisfarne Gospels

You can visit the site of Ad Gefrin today.

St Cuthbert was popular because of his love of people and animals.

How do we know?

Northumbria was a large and powerful kingdom.

Nearly all we know about Anglo–Saxon Northumbria comes from the writings of a monk called Bede. He wrote the first History of the English People in AD 731.

For centuries, nobody knew where Ad Gefrin was until, in 1949, the site near Kirknewton was spotted from an aeroplane.

The Lindisfarne Gospels make up a decorated book written in Latin. For a long time it was kept near the body of St Cuthbert. Today it is in the British Library.

The Longships Arrive

A young girl watches from her hideout in the forest as the boat makes its way up the River Tyne. She has heard that some of these people come to exchange glass, skins and furs for food and drink. But she has also been told that some have destroyed monasteries and killed monks. She must run home to warn her family that the Vikings are on their way.

The Vikings

On 8 June AD 793, Viking invaders from Scandinavia raided Lindisarne, killed the monks and carried off the treasure. Villages along the Northumbrian coast were attacked and terrorized for another 70 years.

Like the Anglo-Saxons before them, the Vikings wanted land to farm and over time they began to settle and marry local people. The Vikings brought with them trade and metalwork skills.

In AD 948, Eric Bloodaxe declared himself King of Northumbria, but Oswulf of Bamburgh wasn't willing to give up his part of the kingdom. He planned an ambush, and Bloodaxe was killed at Stainmore. His death was the end of Viking rule in Northumbria.

'This year came dreadful warnings over the land of the Northumbrians, terrifying the people; these were immense sheets of light rushing through the air, and whirlwinds, and fiery dragons flying across the sky. These terrible events were soon followed by a great famine: and not long after, the horrible attacks of heathen men made awful slaughter in the church of God in Holy-island.'
Entry for the year AD 793 in the Anglo-Saxon Chronicle.

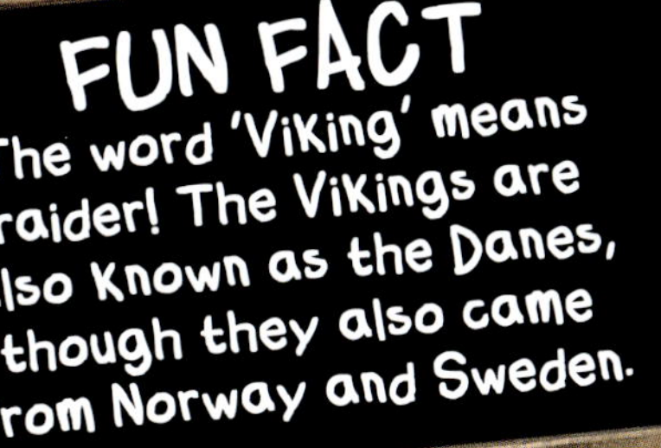

The 1200 year-old Coppergate helmet was found at York in 1982.

How do we know?

We know about the Viking raid on Holy Island because of a letter that was written by a monk called Alcuin to the Northumbrian king and Bishop of Lindisfarne. There is also a dramatic account in the Anglo-Saxon Chronicle. This was a record of England, year by year, kept by monks and scribes. But we have to be careful with these written records as we know that the monks and the Vikings did not get on. The Vikings were not Christians, but had their own gods and myths.

The Vikings left other evidence behind. A number of Viking hoards containing coins and weapons have been dug up in North Yorkshire which was then a part of Northumbria. Most of these finds are now at the Jorvik Centre in York. Nothing similar has been found in Northumberland yet. This might suggest that fewer Vikings settled here.

To Market

William stands in the market square watching the jugglers' amazing tricks. All around him the busy merchants and noisy stallholders are selling their wares. Suddenly the church bell rings. William had better hurry. He is on an errand for his master at Alnwick Castle. He'll be in big trouble if he is late back!

Bamburgh Castle was a backdrop for the 2010 movie 'Robin Hood' starring Russell Crowe.

Castles

When the Normans invaded Britain in 1066, it took them another three years to crush the Northumbrians. This was called the Harrying of the North. Then William the Conqueror set about building castles to defend the border marches between England and Scotland. The two countries could not agree where the border should be, so there was almost constant fighting for the next 300 years.

In the meantime, ordinary Northumbrians carried on farming, raising sheep and cattle, and selling their produce, cloth and leather goods at market. In return for protection from the Marcher Lords, they paid taxes and fought in the Lords' armies.

The Normans also rebuilt the monasteries and abbeys that had been looted by the Vikings or had fallen into neglect. The monks returned to Holy Island, Hexham Abbey and Alnwick Abbey.

...1065 FIRST MENTION OF NORTHUMBERLAND IN THE ANGLO-SAXON CHRONICLE...

Border Wars

There were countless battles between the English and the Scots including two at Alnwick – the first in 1093 and the second in 1134. At the famous Battle of Otterburn in 1388, Henry Percy, Earl of Northumberland, met James Douglas, Earl of Douglas. The English were defeated and 2,000 soldiers were wounded or killed.

These were tough times for Northumberland. Between 1200 and 1300 the towns of Berwick-upon-Tweed, Hexham and Corbridge were all burnt to the ground!

How do we know?

The markets that we visit today in Morpeth, Alnwick, Berwick and Hexham have a long history. Morpeth market charter was granted by King John in 1199 – over 800 years ago. More than 70 castles have been counted in Northumberland. The castles at Alnwick, Bamburgh and Warkworth are still in good condition. Only the ruins of others, such as Dunstanburgh and Norham, remain to be explored. The railway station at Berwick stands on the site of a castle.

There are many songs and poems about the battles of the Marcher Lords, including the 'Ballad of Chevy Chase', which tells the story of the Battle of Otterburn:

Of fifteen hundred Englishmen
Went home but fifty-three;
The rest were slain in Chevy Chase
Under the greenwood tree.

Hexham Hit

Friar James is praying that the king's soldiers will not destroy the abbey. After all, it is the friar's home as well as God's place. It has stood in this place since Queen Etheldreda gave the land to Saint Wilfrid over 850 years earlier. The friar has heard that the king will sell their land and all their treasures so he has hidden Saint Wilfrid's sacred cup and hopes that the soldiers do not find it.

Henry VIII made himself head of the church in England.

Hexham Abbey is still a place of worship today.

Rising of the North

The Tudor King Henry VIII fell out with the Catholic Pope in Rome. He made himself head of the church in England and, in 1537, closed monasteries such as Hexham Abbey. Many were completely destroyed, their treasures taken and some sold as houses to Henry's friends.

Henry's split with the church in Rome caused more problems for Northumberland. Apart from the argument about the England/Scotland border, there was a new argument. Should the country be Protestant or Catholic?

Henry's daughter, Elizabeth I, became queen in 1558. She was also a Protestant. Her cousin, Mary Queen of Scots, was a Catholic and many Catholics, such as Thomas Percy, the Earl of Northumberland, thought she should be queen instead of Elizabeth. In 1569, Thomas Percy rebelled against Elizabeth in the Rising of the North, but Elizabeth's troops outnumbered the rebels and he was defeated. Percy was eventually beheaded at York in 1572.

Pele Towers

By this time, Northumberland had become a lawless no-man's land. Men called reivers made up raiding parties, crossing the border to steal cattle. Families across Northumberland set up their own small armies to protect themselves, their houses and their cattle. They built mini-castles called pele towers which usually had four floors. The ground floor was used to keep the cattle away from the raiders. The peles had few, small windows.

The border was guarded by Wardens of the Marches who were very powerful. Reivers arrested by the Wardens could be fined, jailed, hanged or sent abroad. Couples were not allowed to marry someone from across the border without the Warden's permission.

FUN FACT
In 1587, Archie Graeme and Mary Fenwick were hanged in Haltwhistle for marrying without permission.

A New King

In 1603, James VI of Scotland became James I of England and the two countries were finally united. This marked the beginning of a much quieter time for the people living on Northumberland's borders.

Monasteries were great places of learning, so once they were gone, new schools were needed. King Edward VI Grammar School was set up in Morpeth in 1552 and named after Henry's son. Only boys from rich families were sent there. Here is an imaginary account from John Forster written by candlelight at the top of the family pele tower.

1554

I have spent the whole day at school reciting Latin verbs. When I arrived home, there was panic as word had reached my father that the Lisle family was seen riding down from the Cheviot Hills. If they think they are going to take our herds once more, they had better think again! Father has sent for his friend Sir Ralph Fenwick and I believe the Charltons, Dodds and Milburns are on their way too. In the meantime, I had to round up the cattle and sheep closer to home. Now it is almost midnight, and we're safely locked into the pele tower. I would be grateful for a little peace and quiet so that I can finish my homework!

FUN FACT
The White Cross near Denwick is said to mark a plague burial ground.

Steep, spiral stairs inside the pele tower made it easier to defend.

How do we know?

You can see Saint Wilfrid's cup in Hexham Abbey as Henry VIII's soldiers didn't find it! Northumbrian families such as the Collingwoods, Herons, Grays and Forsters fortified their homes and farms and many of their pele towers can still be seen around Northumberland today. Many of the reivers ended up in court, in jail or on the end of the hangman's noose and their stories appear in official Tudor documents.

The Border Ballads tell some of their stories too. These were often sung or spoken and passed on from person to person and carried from place to place.

Stagecoach!

Mr Joshua Briggs is about to join the stagecoach outside a Northumbrian coaching inn. He is on an early stage of his journey home from Edinburgh to London and has rested overnight with the other passengers. Sadly he has lost one of his bags. It seems to have come off the coach when it hit one of the many bumps on the road. He is asking the innkeeper to put an advert in the local paper to see if anyone has found it.

Bonnie Prince Charlie was known as the Young Pretender.

Further Faster

There were a number of post roads through Northumberland carrying mail and passengers from Newcastle to Edinburgh. One road ran through Corbridge. The other road went to Morpeth then split into the coast road through Berwick-upon-Tweed and the inland road through Wooler. Many of these places still have the old coaching inns today.

One of the best and fastest roads was the military road built by General Wade. It was built after a rebellion by Jacobites in 1745 to move soldiers quickly across the country. The Jacobites were supporters of Bonnie Prince Charlie who wanted to claim the throne from King George II.

SPOT THIS!

Can you spot the Angel Inn at Corbridge where travellers have stayed since 1726?

...1715 FIRST JACOBITE REBELLION...1745 SECOND JACOBITE REBELLION...

Strawberry Fair

With its miles of rolling hills, Northumberland was a great place for raising sheep and cattle. Many men and women worked as labourers on the farms and lived in cottages provided by the landowners. Women were often paid in wool or yarn, which they used to make clothes. Farmers drove their animals to the markets in towns such as Morpeth. You could buy lobsters from Seahouses, kippers from Craster, salt from Blyth, strawberries from Alnwick, leather gloves from Hexham. In the spring and autumn workers flocked to the hiring fairs to sell their services as farm labourers or servants.

Warkworth market cross

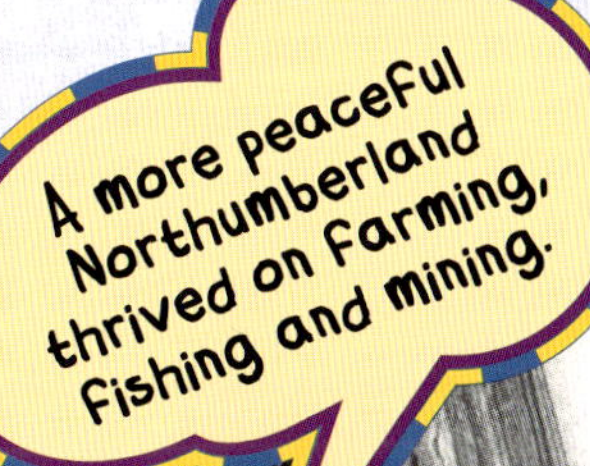

How do we know?

You can still travel along Wade's military road which runs along the line of Hadrian's Wall. Some people at the time wrote about their journeys through Northumberland by stagecoach and Mr Briggs's story is based on one of these tales.

The Topographical Dictionary of England 1848 tells us about the market and fairs in Alnwick: 'The market, abundantly supplied with corn and provisions, is held on Saturday: fairs for cattle and horses are held on May 12th, the last Monday in July, and the first Tuesday in October; and there are other fairs, on the first Saturday in March and in November, for hiring servants.'

Shipyards

It is 1890. The men are hard at work building a new screw-propeller steamship at Blyth. The carpenter is sawing wood to fit out the inside of the ship. Even in this new age of steam, the ship will have a mast and sails to use when there is plenty of wind.

Grace Darling came from Bamburgh.

Fish and Ships

For centuries villages such as Amble, Craster and Seahouses along Northumberland's long coastline made their living from fishing. Fishermen unloaded the fish from their flat-bottomed coble boats for the fishlasses on the harbourside to clean before selling them. Some fish, such as herring, were smoked so that they would keep longer. As the towns grew, so did the demand for fish and the railways made it easy to move fresh fish quickly.

The railways were built to bring coal from the mines to the ports along the coast. In Blyth, coal ships, called 'colliers', were built to carry coal. By 1900, up to three million tons of coal was shipped from Blyth each year.

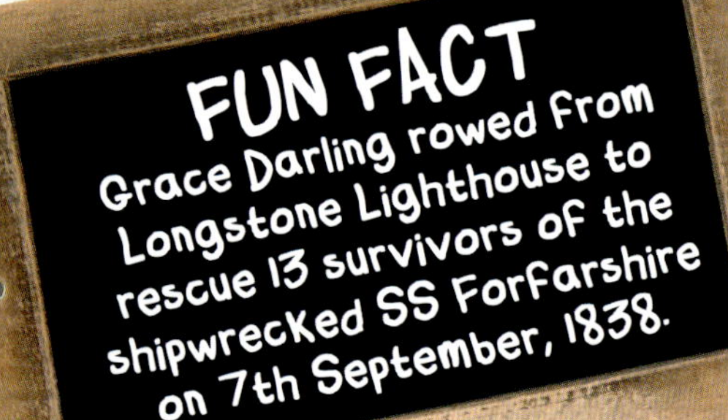

FUN FACT
Grace Darling rowed from Longstone Lighthouse to rescue 13 survivors of the shipwrecked SS Forfarshire on 7th September, 1838.

...1818 GEORDIE LAMP INVENTED...1838 GRACE DARLING'S SEA RESCUE...

Mining

North of Newcastle coal mining was booming but it was dangerous work – gases underground could explode if a miner's candle lamp ignited them. George Stephenson, who was born in Wylam and had worked at Wylam Colliery, invented a miner's safety lamp in 1818. This made coal mines safer places. Even so, 204 miners lost their lives at Hartley, near Blyth, in 1862. The shaft became blocked when heavy machinery collapsed. Lead was mined near Allendale. Lead miners did not face the danger of gas but their mines were very damp and the lead poisonous.

Steam

George Stephenson began building steam locomotives for hauling coal to the surface. His son, Robert, was also an engineer and the Stephensons produced an engine called the Rocket which won a famous race in 1829. Soon after, the Newcastle to Carlisle Railway was built. You can still see the amazing Lambley Viaduct which carried coal and lead over the South Tyne River to Haltwhistle.

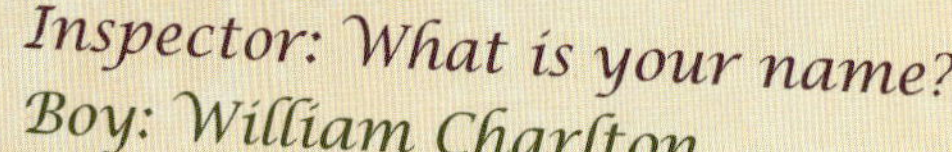

This imaginary account is based on an interview with a young lad called William Charlton who works at Cramlington Colliery.

Inspector: What is your name?
Boy: William Charlton.

Inspector: And how old are you?
Boy: I have just turned 11.

Inspector: And what do you do down the coal mine?
Boy: I'm a foal, sir.

Inspector: And what exactly does a foal do?
Boy: I help the putter to push the wagon full of coal when it is too heavy for him to push it by himself.

Inspector: And who pays you?
Boy: The putter, sir. He gives me fourpence ha'penny out of every shilling he earns – that's if we push along the flat. If we push up hill then the master gives me the money.

Inspector: Do you want to work down the mine for the rest of your life?
Boy: No, sir. My putter, who is 20 years old, goes to night school and is learning to be an engineer. I wouldn't mind doing the same when I am old enough.

CHOLERA Morbus.

THE London Gazette of FRIDAY, contains an Official Document, issued by the Board of Health for the prevention of this Dreadful Disorder, the MAYOR OF NEWCASTLE, particularly requests, that the Inhabitants of this Town, and more especially in the narrow Chares, and Streets, will observe the greatest CLEANLINESS, and that they will open their WINDOWS, and Ventilate their Houses, during the Day.

Mansion House
Oct. 24th, 1831.

Cholera epidemics were caused by dirty drinking water.

The Cholera Inquiry Commission of 1854 reported that in Newcastle alone:

'...during the late outbreak of cholera there, upwards of 1500 persons perished in about nine weeks out of a population of about 90,000...'

FUN FACT
Ashington was once the largest mining village in the world.

A putter and trapper work underground.

How do we know?

We know about working in the mines from a government report of 1842. Government inspectors interviewed men, women and children who worked in the mines. Drawings were made to show the working conditions of the children. Children as young as four or five worked as trappers, opening and closing doors. Children over six years old were working as putters pushing heavy coal wagons. The report was so shocking that the laws were changed so that women and children were not allowed to work down a mine and children had to be given some education. You can find out what it was like to be a miner at the Woodhorn Museum.

Sailors on the old sailing ships sang sea shanties to help them work. 'What Shall We Do With the Drunken Sailor' and 'Billy Boy' are known to have been sung by Blyth sailors.

Evacuate!

Jane and Norman stand in the kitchen of a farmhouse just outside Berwick-upon-Tweed. They have just arrived there from the railway station. They have been sent to a strange house with people they don't know and they don't know how long they will be staying. But it is safer here than at home in Newcastle now that war has broken out. Nobody will bomb Berwick, they hope!

Air Raids

Thousands of children and some adults were evacuated from big cities when World War Two broke out in 1939. The huge shipyards in Newcastle made it a target for enemy aircraft. In 1944, children were evacuated from the south of England to Northumberland. Some children had never lived in the countryside before.

Northumberland made a big contribution to the war effort. The Royal Northumberland Fusiliers were in the thick of the action while fighter aircraft took off from RAF Acklington. While the men were at war, the women who stayed behind took over their jobs. Land girls kept the harvest going to feed the nation.

Britain had to grow its own food during World War Two.

After the War

Many of the big old industries such as coal mining and ship building have been replaced by off-shore wind farms and new, smaller industries. Farming is still very important and Blyth is still a busy port. During the late 1960s and 1970s a new town was built at Cramlington and a big reservoir at Kielder.

FUN FACT
Clothes and food were in short supply during the war so people were given ration books to make sure that everyone had a fair share.

How do we know?

We are lucky to have people alive today who were evacuated as children and can tell us what it was like for them. Photographs from the time and newsreel films shown in cinemas give us an idea of what life was like in wartime. But these were often made to lift people's spirits and didn't show the worst things that were happening. Newspapers, posters and leaflets also give us information about wartime Northumberland.
A group of Ashington colliers painted pictures of the pit villages where they lived and worked. They became known as the Pitman Painters.

Today and Tomorrow

Northumberland has come a long way since the Romans arrived 2,000 years ago. We know how it has changed thanks to objects dug from the ground, written records, old maps and paintings and the many historical buildings that survive. So how will people know about today's Northumbrians in the future?

Jackie Milburn from Ashington played football for Newcastle United and England. Who would you put up a statue to?

Old coble fishing boats have been turned upside down and reinvented as sheds.

You can find out about Longstone Lighthouse and Grace Darling at the Museum, in Bamburgh.

Farmers still show their best animals and produce at the Northumberland County Show held every year at Corbridge. Today, alpacas are on show alongside traditional breeds. What animals will farmers show in the future?

FUN FACT

Northumberland is stuffed with history. There are 200 listed buildings and 45 Iron Age hillforts in Northumberland National Park alone!

⬆ Morpeth Chantry Bagpipe Museum celebrates the music of Northumberland and the skills of Northumbrian pipers such as Kathryn Tickell.

⬆ Thomas Bewick's *History of British Birds* is a fine record of wildlife in the 1700s. Today, Northumberland National Park protects wildlife habitats for the future.

⬆ You can find out what it was like to work in the coal mines at Woodhorn Museum.

⬅ Alnwick Castle's famous gardens were first designed by Capability Brown in 1750. Will they still be enjoyed 250 years from now?

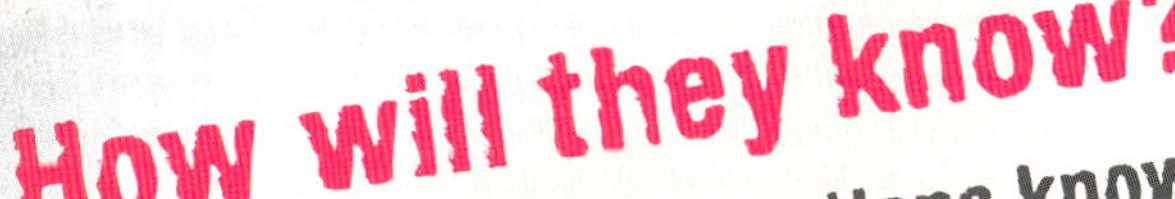

How will they know?

How will future generations know what Northumberland was like for us, now? The internet is a great way of recording the present. Photos, blogs and stories from tourists can all spread the word about our wonderful coastline and countryside. Hundreds of years from now someone may be looking at your picture or reading your blog. You're making history!

Glossary

Abbey – a building where monks or nuns live and work. An abbot is in charge of monks, an abbess is in charge of nuns.

AD – a short way to write anno Domini, which is Latin and means 'in the year of Our Lord', i.e. after the birth of Christ.

Air raid – during World War Two, enemy planes dropped bombs on Britain. This was an air raid.

Archaeologist – a person who studies the past by examining buildings and objects left behind by previous people and cultures.

Catholic – a follower of the Christian religion who considers the pope to be the head of its church.

Charter – written permission to do something. It is often a Royal Charter, meaning the king or queen has given permission.

Cholera – a deadly disease caused by filthy water.

Christian – a person who follows the teachings of Jesus Christ.

Christianity – the name of the religion whose followers believe Jesus Christ is the son of God.

Evacuate – having to leave your home and live somewhere else for safety.

Friars – male members of the Roman Catholic religion. There were Grey Friars, White Friars, Black Friars and Austin Friars.

Hoard – a pile of something valuable hidden away, often used to describe treasure, especially coins.

Knucklebones – another name for a game called 'Jacks', where pieces of stone, bone or metal are thrown and picked up.

Latin – the language of ancient Rome and the foundation of many other languages.

Memorial – something created to make sure we remember the dead or an important past event.

Monastery – a place where monks live and worship.

Monk – a male member of a religious community that has rules of poverty, chastity and obedience.

Pele tower – a fortified tower house which was also a watchtower. A signal fire would be lit on the roof to warn of raids.

Plague – a disease that spreads easily and can kill. In medieval times plague could wipe out thousands of people. It was also called the Black Death.

Pope – the official name for the man who heads the Roman Catholic Church. The Pope lives in the Vatican in Rome.

Protestant – a member of the Christian religion that considers the king or queen of England to be the head of its church.

Ration book – during World War Two, certain food was scarce and had to be rationed. Your Ration Book showed how much of this food you could have every week.

Scribe – a person who made hand-written copies of books, before printing was invented.

Standard bearer – the person who carried the standard (flag) into battle, usually on a pole.

Stylus – a hard writing tool shaped like a pencil but had no lead in it. It was used to write on a wax tablet (see below).

Wax tablet – wax, spread on a wooden board, was soft enough to write on with a pointed stylus.

Wind farm – a place where large groups of windmills are used to create electricity.

Index

Acknowledgements

The publishers would like to thank the following people and organizations
for their permission to reproduce material on the following pages:

p4: Robert Harding World Imagery/Alamy; p5: Putney9/Wikipedia; p7: Jean Hall/Alamy, Les Gibbon/Alamy; p9: Steve Smith/Shutterstock; p13: p13: York Archaeological Trust, www.jorvik-viking-centre.co.uk; p14: Darren Turner/ Shutterstock, Philip Bird/Alamy; p16: Verityjohnson/Shutterstock; p17: Gail Johnson/Shutterstock, Steven Fruitsmaak/ Wikipedia; p19: Tullie House Museum and Art Gallery Trust, Carlisle; Angelo Hornak/Alamy; p20: Woodhorn Museum and Northumberland Archives; p21: Leslie Garland Picture Library/Alamy; p23: Gail Johnson/Shutterstock, S. Forster/Alamy; p25: World History Archive/Alamy; p27: Angelo Hornak/Alamy; p28: Islandstock/Alamy, Darren Turner/Shutterstock, Northumberland County Show; p29: Gail Johnson/Shutterstock, Darren Turner/Shutterstock, Tony Brindley/Shutterstock, History of British Birds Thomas Bewick 1847, Ian Ratcliffe/Shutterstock

All other images copyright of Hometown World

Written by Keith Gregson
Educational consultant: Neil Thompson
Local history consultant: Neil Tonge
Designed by Sarah Allen

Illustrated by Kate Davies, Dynamo Ltd, Virginia Gray, Tim Hutchinson,
Peter Kent, Leighton Noyes, Nick Shewring and Tim Sutcliffe
Additional photographs by Keith Gregson, Alex Long

First published by HOMETOWN WORLD in 2011
Hometown World Ltd
7 Northumberland Buildings
Bath BA1 2JB

www.hometownworld.co.uk

CELT
500 BC
ROMAN
AD 43–410
ANGLO–SAXON
AD 450–1066
VIKING
AD 865–1066
MEDIEVAL TIMES
1066–1485